D.G. SPARE

GETTING HIRED

The Ultimate Guide to Writing the Perfect Cover Letter, Learn Useful Tips On How to Write That Killer Cover Letter That Would Help You Secure The Job

Descrierea CIP a Bibliotecii Naționale a României
D.G. SPARE
   GETTING HIRED. The Ultimate Guide to Writing the Perfect Cover Letter, Learn Useful Tips On How to Write That Killer Cover Letter That Would Help You Secure The Job / D.G. Spare. – Bucharest: Editura My Ebook, 2020
   ISBN

D.G. SPARE

GETTING HIRED

The Ultimate Guide to Writing the Perfect Cover Letter, Learn Useful Tips On How to Write That Killer Cover Letter That Would Help You Secure The Job

My Ebook Publishing House
Bucharest, 2020

TABLE OF CONTENTS

A BRIEF WORD

Thank you for purchasing your copy of "You're Hired!" and for investing your time. Get excited because you're about to learn the insider tips and tricks for making your cover letter jump off the pile and attract the eyeballs of your prospective employer.

Feel free to print off the pages of this book should you wish to read it in comfort but don't forget to keep a pen handy because this isn't some passive little book designed as nothing more than a good read, this is an interactive book that's going to get you thinking about yourself, your skills your experience to use everything to your advantage so that you will outwit, outsmart and ultimately outplay your competition. I know it sounds like a bad episode of Survivor but that's what's really at stake here, it's a matter of who dares, wins.

Because job hunting can be a stressful time in your life, especially in light of the recent economic downturn which people may find themselves in. Your company may have just recently downsized, restructured, reshuffled, merged or closed its doors. No matter the situation you may have just lost your job. All I can say during this challenging time is to keep hope, keep your head up and keep going because you WILL get another job. Also know that even in some of the most distressing and testing times in our lives they can also be the most invigorating, enlightening and rewarding moments which will draw out all of the resources deep within you never knew you had.

In the coming chapters we're going to be drawing a lot of similarities between sales and marketing and constructing a new, improved cover making it better than it was before and if you've never created one before that's ok too because what you'll gather from the pages to come won't just give you an edge but will have you head and shoulders above the rest.

So get excited, see it as a positive and go out there and conquer.

One more point, you'll notice that in the coming chapters we're going to be drawing a lot of similarities between sales and marketing and cover letters.

If you're wondering what sales and marketing, movies and advertisements have to do with cover letters, all I can say is...everything! the only difference is that the asset, the commodity, the product is YOU! Peeling back the layers, everything in one form or another is marketed in some way. Once you realize this, you can have fun with it and play with the rules a little, be different and to think outside the box.

A quick note about the cover letter

Just like we each have 168 hours a week to either use playing video games or to make billions of dollars, we each have a blank, A4 sized piece of paper to work with. What you fill it with is up to you, and what you fill it with will determine whether you get the interview or not. I want to highlight that we all begin at the same starting point where we end up is determined by how best we use the resources and time given us, how we market ourselves in the best way possible and with the information you're about to devour, will give you that competitive edge over yourcompetition.

So if prior to this your cover letters were a little weak and limp that's all about to change today. You're going to write cover letters that command attention and respect and will ultimately get you the jobs you've always been missing out on, that is until now.

I hope you find this to be an entertaining journey, now let's get started.

INTRODUCTION

It's true what they say, that most people spend so much time actually doing their job, bettering themselves, advancing and progressing, rising through the corporate ranks than to worry about how to best market themselves. In fact, that's the last thing on your mind.

You were too busy working it never crossed your mind what you would do if it all disappeared. While you worked so hard for today you barely spared a thought for tomorrow until you find yourself jobless, the reality hits you like a ton of bricks and you're left re-evaluating your life and where to go to from here.

It can be frightening to find yourself in the position where you have to start over again from scratch and it's not until this point that you truly realize that no job is safe, no matter how long you've worked there, how much of your life you sacrificed for the company at your family's expense or how loyal you were. It wasn't personal, just business.

You need to realize that your job was a part of your life but it wasn't what defined you. It's what you did, not who you were. It's difficult to separate the two when it first happens but it's important to know the difference. You can find another job, you will work again and you'll develop new skills or further grow your current skill set.

When tragic things happen in life we can choose how to react to them. It can be a defining event for our own personal growth and help to bring out our best qualities, more than any job could ever do.

So leave the fear of the unknown behind and embrace the mystery of what's to come next.

Then there are those of you who just want a change of scenery, you want the new job, the new challenge to further stretch your career muscles, you're going to gain so much from this.

All those months and years of accumulating knowledge and experience can be a little daunting to condense it all down to just one page.

How do you know what to put in and what to leave out? Don't worry about the details right for the time being, we'll get there soon enough. For the moment we're going to talk about what a cover letter is, why it's so important and why you absolutely need one.

So, for everyone wanting to get that job, here we go.

THE COVER LETTER
YOUR SNEAK PREVIEW MOVIE TRAILER

So there it is, your entire life up to this point summed up onto one little page A4 sized page, that's all the shot you got, fail to knock their socks off and they'll just move on to the next cover letter on the pile.

It's true how little regard recruiters and employers give the stacks of resumes they receive on a daily basis. It gets to the point where every piece of paper begins to look like the rest, but not yours, you're going to stand out from the bunch and get them to take notice, enough so that it will leave them wanting to know more.

Most people simply don't know how to go about this whole process and are frustrated when they are met with rejection letter after rejection letter. They don't realize that the difference between getting the job and losing out to the next person could be a simple as making a minor change. We're going to learn about some of the things that employers look for that will make your cover letter jump out and grab them by the eyeballs.

So what exactly is a cover letter and why do I need one?

Well, just like the Joker has his calling card, you need one of your own too. Something that sets you apart and distinguishes you from the crowd, only the ace up your sleeve is your cover letter.

A word in short – just how important is that little piece of A4 sized paper we call a cover letter?

Let me put it into perspective for you. It's the single most important piece of real estate squeezed onto an A4 sized piece of paper. It literally has the ability to make or break whether or not you get the job. That's why it pays to put some serious time into perfecting it, much like a winning sales letter or a killer advertizing campaign.

Your cover letter is a summary of your resume designed to grab the reader's attention, highlighting all of the key aspects that make you the ideal candidate and the right person for the job. So, you could call it the distillation of your resume into a condensed version that represents you.

It's amazing this entire book is dedicated to the cover letter alone because of its importance in the chain of events that eventually lead you to the job. The cover letter is the single most influential piece of paper when determining how far in the job process you get because let's face it, you produce an awful cover letter there's not much chance of you getting your resume read or getting the call for the interview, so the cover letter in essence is where it all begins.

We're going to highlight all of the best techniques to go about crafting your cover letter for maximum success.

When it comes to your cover letter, the mindset you need to have is to treat the entire process as a sales advertisement where the product on sale is "you". Every piece of information you submit is designed to pique their interest to get them to want to know more.

In fact to be really specific, your cover letter is more a like 30 second movie trailer. The trailer is the thing that determines whether people will want to commit to the entire movie or not. Your cover letter gives you the opportunity to pre-sell yourself.

Because you have in reality such a short time frame to make an impression get used to working within time constraints. When it comes to crafting your cover letter, what facts should you include at the beginning that will make the most impact? If you had only 30 seconds and only one shot, what would you say? what would you want people to know about you? When you give yourself time limits you place your creativity in a pressure cooker forcing you to get the very best from yourself.

It was believed that applicants had on average around 30 seconds to wow their prospective employers or hiring managers, however with competition and job shortages the time limit is even more brutal, in fact it sits at around the 8 second mark. If you can work within those constraints and become accustomed with it the better off you'll be and the greater edge you'll have over your competitors.

YOU ONLY HAVE 8 SECONDS

Psychologists have found that it only takes an average of 8 seconds for your prospective employer to know or not whether they're going to read your resume. This is true and is based upon basic fundamental psychology because on average, we each require only 8 seconds to make a subconscious decision about something,

Here is the example at play in the real world. When we meet people for the first time our perceptions of them are already formed in the first 8 seconds of meeting them.

When we're walking down the street, our 8-second decision-making process is constantly at play as we judge potential threats from those around us, also known as "gut instinct" or "intuition".

This is a part of the evolutionary process which Is part of the limbic system in the brain that developed over the centuries, a survival mechanism to protect us from danger, also known as fight or flight and the ability to make split second decisions which was most often the difference between life and death.

We still have these traits, although not as heightened as it was for survival yet we still use them on a daily basis when assessing our "risk" to "reward" ratio when it comes to making decisions and you will find that your potential employer is no different.

Not to bore you, just to explain why things are the way they are and if you can get your head around that you can actually start to play with these rules. You can outsmart your competition by being armed with this proprietary information and wow your employer much earlier on in their decision making process.

Everyone seems to have less time on his or her hands these days and prospective employers are no exception. Knowing this fact should retrain the way you think and construct your cover letter. This means not leaving the most important parts of your skill set and relevant experience to the second paragraph, it means packing a punch straight out of the gate.

So think about some of your positive points, if someone only gave you 8 seconds to hear you out, what would you want them to know? Having this knowledge gives you a distinct advantage because it completely changes the way you construct your cover letter by placing all of your attention grabbing information in your first paragraph, which is the most crucial one.

Don't take rejection personally it's all part of the process. People have misconceptions about employers, yes it is their job to weed out the wheat from the tares, it's their job so that they can get the cream of the crop, however they *WANT* to find you. They want to give you the chance to wow them and to make an impression; it's not their life's mission to reject you at every chance although it may often feel like it. They want you to be the one they're looking for, the one who is the best fit for the company and who will add value to it and whose vision, beliefs and ideals ties in with their own.

So show them that, be what they're looking for. Do a little research and homework about the company to find out exactly how you can fit in with their vision and add value and profits to their bottom line.

So remember, rejection isn't personal, they really want you to be the candidate they're looking for to make the frustration and time worth it, they're just waiting for someone amongst the hundreds of cover letters they're wading through to be the one that excites them and ignites their curiosity.

Here's a little exercise you can do right now to kick start the process. You're going to give them the one two punch in the first paragraph. You're going to treat it like the only paragraph they're going to read and if this were the case, what would you write knowing full well that you only had 8 seconds at the most?

When you read your first paragraph try to be objective, would you want to know more about you? Try to put yourself in your potential boss's shoes, what kinds of skills, experience, qualities are they looking for?

Give it to someone else so they can be a voice of reason and give an impartial opinion.

Write 5 different cover letters and give them to family and friends to see which ones jumped out the most to them and then refine them further.

Don't worry if you're struggling with it, this is just an exercise to get the creative juices flowing. I mentioned earlier that it's always somewhat challenging when it comes to pinpointing your own strengths when we spend so little time thinking of them but that's okay, we'll address some great tips to help you identify your strengths in the coming chapters.

So to recap, the first paragraph of your cover letter is the most vital.

Here is a flow diagram to illustrate this point in more detail and how you move up through the ranks:

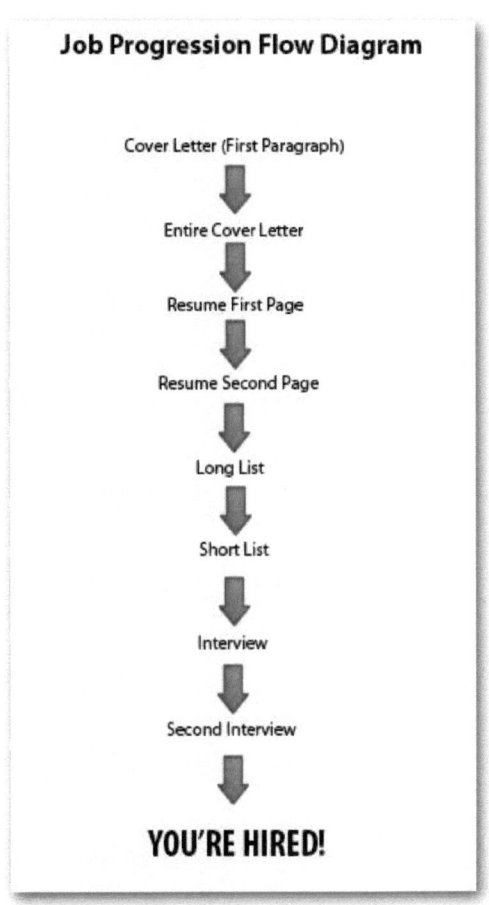

This diagram hits home how important your cover letter really is and how it kicks off the whole process up until the point of getting the job, so listen up, pay attention and take some notes, we're going to be detailing the top rules to help you be the best version of yourself and to capture that cover letter so you'll be at the top of list.

TOP 10 RULES FOR WRITING COVER LETTERS THAT KILL THE COMPETITION

I remember back in my parent's days all you needed to get a job was to turn up. You could literally walk in off the street because there was so much work on hand they were just giving it away. Resumes were never heard of, let alone cover letters.

Unfortunately these days to compete in our current marketplace you need these tools because they provide the basis for job screening for recruiters and potential employers to whittle down the volume of people applying for the job, to get the people they want. Not only are they important to have but also they have become an industry standard and anything less just won't be considered.

We're going to cover 10 of the best tips when writing your cover letter; these will provide valuable guidelines to get the very best out of yours.

Rule 1 - Passion And Enthusiasm

That fire in your belly so to speak. Reach down deep, dig out that primal instinct and go after that job.

Go after what you want and act like you really want it. I know it sounds crazy but it's not. This fire will jump off your letter and touch those reading it. There's nothing wrong with digging deep, go after that job like you really mean it, act like it's the last job on earth and it's already yours and you'll develop the right attitude.

That fire, that energy and enthusiasm will jump off the page and reveal the type of person you are and that you're keen. The right attitude and mindset can open lots of doors and put you above the others just applying for the sake of it.

Give the same energy to each of your cover letters for each job application and you will make the person reading it see something special in you. You will keep this momentum for each cover letter you write too, whether it's for your 1st or your 50th, keep the same energy level because to your boss to be, this is your first cover letter to them not your umpteenth, so approach every cover letter you purposely craft for each position be written through a fresh pair of eyes by tailoring it to suit each job position.

Share your energy and enthusiasm but never be desperate, come from a position of confidence and you will have mass appeal amongst recruiters and prospective employers.

Rule 2 - Know Who You're Writing To

Most people just threw up their hands with how obvious this statement was but think about how many people get this wrong.

I know, it sounds like a no-brainer doesn't it? In actual fact most people trip up on this minor oversight. It goes far beyond just getting the name of the company, the recruitment officer, or the human resources manager right. Certainly addressing the correct person ensures that your cover letter at least gets read by the right person but this goes way beyond just finding out the usual, surface details.

To go a step further and to stand out you need to do what 90% of others aren't prepared to do. While other applicants are spraying their cover letters everywhere hoping that something will stick, posting out their default cover letter with every application they send, but YOU won't be making that mistake.

To get noticed above the others who are not willing to go that extra mile like you will, you're going to do some extra research of your own which goes way beyond just finding the correct person and department.

Always put yourself in the position of your boss to be. They receive so many letters on a daily basis and they know without a doubt who took the time to make the effort and who just wrote them for the sake of putting an extra feeler out there. Taking the time to know who you're writing to will pay off.

So how can you find out about them?

If you're coming in from the cold, do a little investigative research by surfing the Internet. Technology continues to make the world a smaller place and you'll be able to find that almost any company is listed online.

This is a valuable tool you have at your fingertips, so use it. Find out about your prospective employer, about their company, it's background history, how it came to be, are there any interesting points that stand out to you and something you could use in your cover letter or to win you cool points in your interview?

What can you learn about their core values? their business beliefs and how does this tie in with your own?, what you can offer them?, what can you ultimately bring to the table that would make you a good fit for them?

When composing your cover letter always personalize each one specifically for the position you are applying for because they will all differ, no matter how little it's best to customize your cover letter to suit each specific job application, no one cover letter is a one size fits all. That extra attention to detail will always pay off.

Your cover letter qualifies you for the first step to meet the company's minimum requirements for the job and paves the way for the interview. You successfully jump this hurdle will inch you closer to the job finish line.

The rest you sell in the interview, in fact around 70% of the information comes from the interview process alone. This is where they get to experience firsthand your personality and can really gauge if you would be a good fit for their company. They also want to see how your personality would blend with other team members and how it would affect the current working dynamic.

So, do your homework, the extra work will give you the extra edge.

Rule 3 - To the Point

When writing your cover letter, organize your information so that it's easy to read.

The human brain including that of your recruiter's, human resources manager and boss to be, likes simplicity, structure and order.

It helps to structure information in your cover letter with bulleted points.

This makes it readable, draws attention to relevant points and gives it a natural flow on effect.

Presenting your information in bite-sized chunks also makes it easier to process.

You wouldn't try to force feed an entire meal in one mouthful would you? The same applies to how you organize your information.

Smaller pieces of information are easier to digest and absorb and will stand out to your prospective employer. It also makes a statement about you, it shows that you are concise, to the point, structured and well organized. A well-presented and organized cover letter speaks volumes of the person creating it.

Here's how to pack a punch of bite sized information tidbits:

Try using shorter sentences around 15 to 16 words in length. Having sentences 30 words or more in length is the equivalent of someone rambling on about him or herself and not getting the point. This gives the impression the applicant is more interested in talking about themselves, not to mention being hard on the eyes which is a turn off when your employer to be has poured over several applications in the space of a day.

Having too many long paragraphs strains the eyes leaving them to wonder what they're meant to focus on.

The use of bulleted points with plenty of white space gives good eye relief. This is a well-known tactic that sales copywriters use. They leave plenty of white space on either side of the text so that the reader can easily focus on what the writer wants them to, which is to get their sales pitch across.

This work s equally well whether you're trying to sell a product or trying to get an interview, it's all the same. This technique works in every area because we are all human beings meaning that we all respond to the same psychological triggers no matter what the situation, your boss to be included.

You also have to remember that yours is one of many. Employers and recruiters are busy people and they don't have a lot of time. You can guarantee that by the middle of the day that your cover letter could be the 50th on the pile, which is why you want to get the most bang for your buck by writing short and simple sentences. Chances are that your cover letter will find its way into the hands of a recruiter or a screener who may not be all that familiar with your field and so to ensure that you make it past the first hurdle, keep it simple enough so that those screening your cover letter will know how best to forward you on to the proper channels.

Rule 4 - Don't Lie

Your mother was right about not telling tales, and for a very good reason, it will always come back to bite you.

Always tell the truth on your cover letter, your resume and your interview.

Don't think you can bend or twist the truth and not have consequences as a result of it. They will always find out, it's their job to do so and if you get caught lying can be a very embarrassing thing, not to mention if through lying you landed your job can be grounds for immediate dismissal if you get caught. It's not worth it and there's no such thing as grey, only black and white. Don't risk it.

Rule 5 - Keeping It Simple

Keep your language simple and to the point. Write naturally like you would to a regular person. Avoid using stuffy and unnatural language that you wouldn't normally use in your everyday life. You don't want to be a different person on paper than you are in real life.

You want your personality to shine through enough for the interviewer/manager in charge to want to meet you. Just make sure the language you use reflects the real you, after all that's the person they will be drawn to. That's not to say that you shouldn't be unprofessional, writing with personality doesn't give you an excuse to write sloppy language with spelling and grammar errors.

Remember you want to make an impression and even the most enticing cover letters laced with typos can be a huge turn off.

Start by writing like you would directly to the person interviewing you. Visualize them sitting across from you and tell them what you want them to know about you, write those points down.

Write as many as you can, spare nothing, you can always alter and change it later but for now this gets the creative juices flowing. Don't mentally edit your thoughts, let it all flow out on paper. Not only is this good practice to think on your feet but it also helps prepare you for the interview process.

Take all of the points you've just written down, and then flesh out each one. Pick the best 5 to 10 points to use in your cover letter.

Rule 6 - Short „n Sweet

The length of your cover letter should be under a page, 3 to 4 paragraphs at the most, anything over that unless requested should be avoided. Short, sweet and to the point is the order of the day. Long cover letters can make you look longwinded and ultimately get tossed into the bin. Make it a goal to get your point across quickly, always assume they don't have a lot of time and considering the current job market and number of applicants is a fact.

Paragraph 1 – Strong opener, get attention, hook interest
Paragraph 2 – Back up with credentials, skills,
qualifications, experience
Paragraph 3 – Conclusion, call to action

Rule 7 - Tone

Believe it or not but the way you write can influence the impression of you. Each of us has a signature tone in all of our letters. The way you write should be consistent.

Some believe that writing in the third person removes the "I" factor from the equation, for example "generated over 1 million dollars in extra company revenue in 2008".

This way you can humbly boast about your achievements without appearing conceited then compared with "I generated over 1 million dollars in extra company revenue in 2008". The second approach is more personal however if you have a half a dozen bullet points can get a little repetitive and make you look self centered. Mix it up, find the right balance for you and remember it's about what you can bring to the table.

Put yourself under the microscope and highlight your best qualities so that it becomes a focal point and convinces them that you're the person they have to meet.

Rule 8 - Trial By Typo

No typos or grammatical errors, remember the spell check isn't perfect and as the saying goes your computer will do what you tell it to do and not what you want it to. Your employer will use this to profile you, it's all they have to go by before they even meet you.

If your cover letter is full of mistakes, then they will probably deem your work ethic to be along similar lines which means you risk getting through to the next phase and securing yourself the interview. Harsh but true, this is what's really going behind the scenes once your cover letter is received and because you know this you can do something about it to ensure you don't fall into the same trap.

Rule 9 - Attention to Detail

Most people just send out a standard, carbon copy one size fits all cover letter when applying for positions and the person on the receiving end will know this. They will know it's a standard letter and that all was changed were the recipient details because it's too generic, it doesn't talk about the job specifics or how your skills relate to them, in short it gives them nothing to go by, with yours quickly ending up the trash bin.

Think what you would like to receive, you would give greater care and consideration knowing that something was tailor made with you in mind and the details prove this.

When creating your cover letter, outline the job skills they are requesting and how you fit into this. Like a conversation, address some of the points in the application so that they know you really read it. This will not only stand out to your prospective employer but it will set you apart from the rest of the pack.

Treat each cover letter like it's the one that's going to get the job, always pay particular care and attention not to get food or drink stains on it as this speaks volumes about you. Your potential employer may see your sloppy cover letter with smudge or inkblot and get the impression that your work habits are the same and may have doubts about meeting you.

This is the only impression they have to go by so don't take yourself out of the running on a technicality. Pay attention to those little details that paint a picture of you because you only have one chance to make a first impression.

Rule 10 - Change Your Strategy

Just like ad campaigns, great cover letters are made and not born. It takes a little time and testing to know if it's a hit or miss. If you're not getting the response you were hoping for then change elements of your cover letter and then measure your result, in short if it's not working – change it.

Just writing and sending out applications to prospective employers without questioning why a callback or interview isn't forthcoming isn't good enough.

By not sparing a thought of what you're doing or not doing each time a cover letter goes out could be costing you the job.

If it's not working, change it. Any good ad campaign will be honed and fine-tuned until it can't get any better. You need to do the same.

If you're not hearing back, you need to change your strategy. If you're not getting the interview then why? Include or exclude from your cover letter what you need to, make some changes and then look at the results. If you get more callbacks and interviews then you've just created your own perfect campaign cover letter that you can continually use to help get your foot in the door.

If no matter what you do doesn't result in a callback or at the very least a declined application letter then call the company and speak to the person in charge to find out why, this will not only earn you some respect but your initiative will leave a lasting impression of you and possibly even alter their initial opinion of you.

As they say if you keep doing what you're doing you'll keep getting what you're getting. You need to change your strategy, like a finely tuned ad campaign. There is no such thing as luck in this game, you create your own luck through the tactics you use to get noticed.

Think of your letter as a work in progress, it's not your baby and you should be able to change it as often as you need to so don't get attached to it. Test your letters and see which one gets the most response then use that letter and refine it until you get the best letter you possibly can.

Rule 11 - It's Not All About You

You know whom I'm talking about, those annoying people that you meet that talk of nothing other than themselves. When you write your cover letter be sure to not just focus on yourself but rather how your skills and experience can be of value to the company potentially hiring you. Address your employers needs rather than focusing solely on what you want to get out of the situation. What's in it for them? can you increase performance, productivity and profits?

Rule 12 - Follow Up

Always follow up by phone, email or by snail mail if your resume and cover letter was received. After an interview, thank you letters provide additional information they may find valuable in the decision to hire you. This is the stuff that most others won't do, your competition prefers to do the bare minimum to hopefully get by, but not you. You want that job and you're going to get it so as with anything in life if you want success, you have to do what 99% of the crowd aren't prepared to do and that's to invest the time, effort and energy into your purpose. By creating new, positive habits, the success will come in anything you do.

KNOW THYSELF - WHAT YOUR POTENTIAL EMPLOYER IS LOOKING FOR

You Under the Spotlight – time to do a little soul searching and self reflection

Know Thyself – if you've ever seen the movie The Matrix you'll understand this expression, although it was originally coined by the Greek philosopher Socrates. When you know yourself, you can spot your strengths.

Most people don't give their strengths and positive traits a second thought however now is not the time to be shy, you have to pull every resource from within you in the form of a brain dump, everything and anything you can think of, then you can be more selective when editing your list by weeding out the traits and skills that aren't of particular relevance for the job you're applying for.

You The Product – How To Unearth Your Strengths

This is where all of the general knowledge is about you. You're going to know yourself better than ever before as you determine your strengths that will give you the competitive edge.

To get the very best out of yourself and to put your best foot forward you need to know what your strengths are.

It's hard to often see this in ourselves but our best judge can often be those around us. Talk to family and friends to see what some of your strengths are and list them.

Even in situations where you helped to resolve conflict, this could come in handy with your job interview, as this always seems to be a popular question that often crops up.

You could ask how about a situation where you showed good leadership and management skills, jog your memory for workplace applications of these attributes.

Here is a worksheet to help get you thinking. You'll find some specifics about how your skills can be a benefit and an asset to your prospective employer.

Your Strengths	Benefits to your employer
Organized	Save company money with increased efficiency
Good Salesperson	Increase company's revenue and bottomline
Time Management	Punctual and efficient employee

Translate your strengths into real world benefits for your employer so that they can get an idea of how you'd be a good fit for their company. Remember, they're constantly trying to find how your skills would merge in with their company's vision and this a great way to start thinking along those lines.

Questions To Help Identify Your Strengths

1. List your last 3 jobs including your current one or your most recent one:

1. Job title and year

_____

2. Job title and year

_____

3. Job title and year

_____

2. For each job position what abilities and skills did you need to possess in order to do your job well?

1.

_____

_____

_____

_____

_____

2.

_____

_____

_____

_____

_____

3.

_____

_____

_____

_____

_____

What challenges did you face in each job position and how did you attempt to resolve them?

1.

_____

_____

_____

_____

_____

_____

2.

_____

_____

_____

_____

_____

3.

_____

_____

_____

_____

_____

What was the outcome? was it an increase in profits?, did you save money as a result of your action?, was it a conflict resolution?

1.

_____
_____
_____
_____
_____

2.

_____
_____
_____
_____
_____

3.

_____
_____
_____
_____
_____

Did you get any positive verbal or written feedback from your superior or even your co-workers as a result of the actions you took?

1.

_____

_____
_____
_____
_____
_____

2.
_____

_____
_____
_____
_____
_____

3.

_____

_____
_____
_____
_____
_____

How did you best benefit the company/s you worked for? what leadership skills did you exhibit? Did you work well as part of a team?

1.

_____

_____
_____
_____
_____

2.

_____

_____
_____
_____
_____

3.

_____

_____
_____
_____
_____

What are some of your personal strengths?

_____

_____

_____

_____

_____

_____

What are some of your most notable character traits others have shared with you?

_____

_____

_____

_____

_____

What are some of your weaknesses?

_____

_____

_____

_____

_____

Print this section off and give to family, friends and colleagues.

You need to be objective here, don't take offence. This is an exercise in character building and you need as much information about yourself as possible and the majority of the time we don't see ourselves the way that others do. You may be able to pinpoint your best traits but perhaps others can see even more of them than you can.

Perhaps you have things that you could work on to make you an even better person for the job.

If we have weaknesses then it's good to identify, not to focus and dwell on but to turn into strengths. This could arise in your interview and if you know what your weaknesses are, you can address them and tell them how you're resolving and working through it.

Employers eat this up, why? Because **NOBODY** is perfect. By not divulging any weaknesses when asked makes them a little nervous because you haven't revealed anything about yourself that makes you human and allows them to connect with you. Being aware of your weaknesses shows character, you know you're only human but that it's admirable that you are working on those issues.

So pick which weaknesses you want to share. You need to have a couple though this shows you're in touch with yourself and that you're working on them to become an even better individual.

So don't get offended if family or friends point out some things you may have been unaware of.

It's going to help you in your interview, you're not going to mention these weaknesses in your cover letter or resume, you don't want to write yourself out of the game before you even get started. Bare in mind the interview because it's bound to crop up.

Only give this to trusted family and friends, people with whom you have a rapport and a relationship with, people that know you well enough to paint a clear picture of you.

This section is of particular interest if you have gaps in your work history or have been a stay at home mom for a while. Being out of action for a while in the wok realm doesn't mean that you haven't obtained the equivalent in life experience so this will help to get the ball rolling.

THIS SECTION TO BE FILLED BY FAMIILY AND FRIENDS

I'm approaching you to help me fill in information about myself from your perspective. I've chosen you because I trust you and have known you for a long time. Your feedback is welcomed and appreciated.

Please fill this honestly, you're only helping me to dig out my best so that I can use it to my advantage and if I need to change anything it only helps me to build character and to become a better person.

54

1. What are my strengths?

_____

_____

_____

_____

_____

2. How could these be considered an advantage in a workplace scenario?

_____

_____

_____

_____

_____

3. What are my best qualities?

_____

_____

_____

_____

_____

1. How could these be considered an advantage in a workplace scenario?

_____
_____
_____
_____
_____
_____

2. Has there been a situation where I exhibited leadership traits during a crisis?

_____
_____
_____
_____
_____
_____

3. How do I handle situations of stress?

_____
_____
_____
_____
_____
_____

4. How can I learn to manage this in a more effective way?

_____

_____
_____
_____
_____
_____

5. How do I handle conflict resolution?

_____

_____
_____
_____
_____
_____

6. How can I learn to manage this in a more effective way?

_____

_____
_____
_____
_____
_____

7. What are two things I could improve upon and do better?

_____

_____

_____

_____

_____

8. Is there anything other information that would be useful in a work setting? for example my time management skills, attention to detail, professionalism, hard working and dedication, personality and people skills, etc.

_____

_____

_____

_____

_____

Thank you for taking the time to fill in this questionnaire. It was greatly appreciated.

Does this give you an idea of some of your strengths through situations and dealings with your fellow co-workers?

Just listing everything that springs to mind will hopefully help jog your memory and get you recalling lots of things you've achieved in the past but probably forgot.

Write as many as you can and then narrow it down to the top 5, but keep a mental note of them all, they may come in handy during the interview should they fire questions at you and you need a quick answer.

THE SCIENCE BEHIND BUILDING
THE ULTIMATE COVER LETTER

Even the bionic man was made of superhuman, robotic parts. He was smashed to pieces but then was rebuilt one piece at a time to become bigger, better, faster.

You have to treat your cover letter in the same way. Forget everything you knew about cover letter writing. We're going to take your old rehashed, good for nothing old cover letter, smash it to pieces and rebuild it from the ground up making it bigger, better and ahem...faster, you get the idea.

So how do you rebuild from the grass roots up? you need to start from the beginning.

Before you even write a single character you need to know the subtleties of the human psyche. Advertisers for long have exploited this fact, they know your weak points and your psychological triggers and they take advantage of them.

How else do you think they were able to convince generations of people to believe that smoking didn't just invigorate you but that it also improved your attractiveness, virility and confidence? We all know the associated dangers and health risks that come with smoking these days, but it's incredible what nations of people were conned into believing.

This is great selling and whether you know it or not, the human brain hasn't really evolved much over the past few centuries to hit home this point, we still respond to these same emotional triggers today which if you like, fall into the 7 deadly sins mentality.

We can all have our lust and greed pandered to and just look at all the instant quick fix products strewn all over the market these days that promise beauty in a jar and instant weight loss while sitting on your couch watching television. If that doesn't appeal to the sloth in us then I don't know what does.

Your employer is no different; we are going to appeal to their emotional triggers too by using what has worked in the advertising arena for years.

Every piece of advertising material must cater to 4 basic rules in order to truly be successful and your cover letter is no different, don't forget that.

Your cover letter needs to have these 4 main ingredients to enjoy the same kind of success a lucrative marketing campaign does, only the end result is the job you want.

This is known as:

- **Attention**
- **Interest**
- **Desire**
- **Action**

Attention

You need to grab your employer's attention immediately. There is little room for error when it comes to this and must be done purposefully with the intention of taking the job process further.

So how do you do this?

1. Stationery Choice

Before you even get your cover letter opened, particularly in cases where you are sending a snail mail version, the choice of stationery says a lot of about you before reading a single word. You can grab instant attention by purchasing good quality paper and envelopes that match. This makes a good impression, shows your serious about the job and are have given much thought and consideration into every aspect of your application, even right down to the finer points of your stationery choice. It also sets the standard of what your employer expects. If you look the part professionally, you have more credibility with the expectation your cover letter and resume to be of similar professional quality making it worth their while to open your application.

2. Clean „n Tidy

This not only demonstrates that you have approached the matter in a professional way but it also reflects on the kind of person that you are. Remember they have nothing to judge you by. They've never met you in person or spoken to you over the phone and in terms of first impressions, this is it. So it's important to keep your envelope and stationery coffee and egg stained free. You don't want to send mixed messages by having top-notch stationery with this morning's breakfast smeared all over it. What kind of message are you sending of yourself if your enveloped is covered in food or smudge marks? believe it or not, it can reflect poorly on you making them view your work ethic in a similar light.

3. To Whom It May Concern

Another attention getter that seems so simple is addressing the envelope. Make sure that you address it to the correct person, department and company and that it's free of spelling errors. Don't write a generic title, look it up online or call up reception and get the information personally if you have to, the little time taken to research this little detail will pay off big time.

Which would you rather receive?

Attention: Charles Miller has a more professional ring to it than say…

Attention: To Whom It May Concern. That personal touch gets your cover letter opened and read.

Interest

The next phase in your cover letter campaign is to gain their interest. We've passed the first hurdle; the professional demeanor of your envelope got their attention so now we need to get them interested in what we have to say.

The best way to go about this is to demonstrate your company knowledge. Again, researching you can garner plenty of information online. This shows your attention to detail and that you care about the company you're applying to.

Drop detail that shows you've done your homework, for example what past achievements has attracted you to apply in the first place? How are your skills a match for the company and how could they best be used?

You can open with something like:

Dear Mr. Brown,

Upon further researching your company, I found a fascinating editorial published online in the New York Times dated December 3rd 2008. What I realized is that I want to be apart of your innovative and inspiring team and that I have the skills to help drive the spirit of ingenuity further forward.

You can include excerpts in your cover letter or enclose a copy of the article as part of your application. You can also attach it as part of your email cover letter. If you can't find any write-ups online or in magazines or in your local newspaper pertaining to the company, simple investigation of the company web site online would suffice. Being able to mention details about their policies, history and background always impresses.

You can always call reception and ask for those details yourself if information online is vague or sparse.

Desire

Just like a commercial where you've hooked their attention, you want to then appeal to their desire to know more. This is another step on the ladder moving you closer to the interview and ultimately the job. It's at this stage they get a clearer picture of you, your credentials, skills, personality and whether or not you're a good fit for their company.

To create desire, back up your claims with evidence, this includes your credentials that support why you would be a good fit for the job.

Don't forget as with our opener which was designed to create interest it was all about grabbing eyeballs by making a statement "you should consider me and look not further because….", "I increased my current companies revenue by 12%", "I restructured and streamlined our companies present processes and cut down on wasted staff productivity and sick leave days". Now what's left to do is drive that point home with fact that backs up your original "interest" getting statement.

> **For example: I have an MBA from the University of Chicago with a major in marketing.**
>
> **Because your company is goal orientated, I consider myself to be someone that gets results. As you will see from my resume, I have reached and surpassed all targets set forth by the company I last worked for and am completely confident I can bring the same skills, knowledge and drive to your company.**

Action

Just as it suggests, action is all about your employer acting upon your cover letter. They've passed through all the steps from initially opening your cover letter to liking what they see, now you want them to take action by getting them to contact you.

You can achieve this by giving enough information in your cover letter to motivate them to read your resume.

This means giving just the right amount of information with out giving away the farm. It's about maintaining the balance of giving away just enough to pique their curiosity to know more so that they'll have to pick up the phone and speak to you inperson.

Don't be afraid to ask for the interview, you only get what you want in life if you ask for it. Most applicants' leave it open ended where they "hope for the best". Most don't even have the decency of receiving a token rejection letter by not hearing anything at all. Make your actions clear, you applied to get the job, so ask for it.

Don't leave it to chance. Chances are you ask for an interview, you'll probably get it because it showed confidence and initiative on your part.

End your cover letter proactively and boldly by having it lead to the interview, after all isn't that the whole purpose of the cover letter?

So don't end a genius cover letter with leaving your employer hanging. Get that interview, they'll be more than willing if you play your cards right to give you the interview, remember they want to find you.

Some great closers for your cover letter

I would like to meet with you in person to discuss matters further..."

"I will talk in greater depth about how I achieved an 11% sales growth during our last business quarter and how I plan to achieve that for xyz company".

"I look forward to meeting you in person and how I can be of service to the xyz corporation".

"I have done some background research on your company and feel you could save money with a few ideas I have. With your permission I would like the opportunity to meet in person with you to discuss these ideas in greater detail. I think you might like what I have in mind".

"I will contact you on the October 12th 2009 to arrange a meeting time with you"

"To really demonstrate that I am the best possible candidate for the job I would like to arrange a meeting with you".

"Appreciate your time and look forward to hearing from you in the near future.

The cover letter winners seal the deal by taking the necessary action. Not content for the employer to get back to you when it suits leaves plenty of room for uncertainty. Suggesting that you will follow up shows initiative and puts a deadline on things for you. This way if the outcome didn't swing your way you can move on to the next job position without being left wondering.   Not content for the employer to get back to you when it suits leaves plenty of room for uncertainty. Suggesting that you will follow up shows initiative and puts a deadline on things for you. This way if the outcome didn't swing your way you can

You continue to hone and perfect the art of crafting topnotch cover letters and it'll be like an army of cover letters out there doing the work for you. All that's left to do is turn up to the interview.

BUILDING A COVER LETTER WITH AN UNFAIR ADVANTAGE OVER THE COMPETITION

Now that you know the basic structure of a cover letter and the successful elements that go into making it an exceptional, stand out piece, here's a little writing exercise to start building a kick butt cover letter of your own.

How To Give Your Cover Letter The Rock Star Treatment

Because the first paragraph is the most vital, you need to practice perfecting this.

We're going to do this by getting you to practice writing short, concise paragraphs that pack a punch.

Here a few ideas to get the ideas flowing, mix and match them. You'll see a common theme amongst them all, they pack a quick punch that hooks the employer into reading more. You absolutely need this with fleeting attention spans and with hundreds of other applicants to pour through.

Rather than the typical

Dear Sir/Madam,

I am applying for the position of Legal Secretary found in the West Haven Tribune on the 15th of August 2009.
I feel my current skills are a good fit for the job position and have enclosed a copy of my resume with my application for the position.

Personally that opener makes me sleepy and chances are they'll think so too, especially when yours doesn't stand out of a bunch of snoozers.

You're going to grip them immediately because you have to, it's all the time you have to wow them, so use it to your advantage.

You're going to use:

Dear Ms Roberts,

I am fully aware that you have several applicants vying for the position of Executive Sales Manager. However, I would like you to know why I think I am the person for the job and why you should contact me first.

Increasing my company's profits by 11% in the previous fiscal year and being on target to nearly double that figure puts me in a position to be a very valuable asset to your company. I know I can do the same for _____ and would relish the challenge in doing

Now if you were the employer you would definitely want to call this person over the first application and that is literally what happens. This is how they choose; this is why you don't get the call. Someone else presented what they had better than you, even if you know that you're more qualified for the position. It's the person that gets their cover letter read, and acted upon that gets the jobs.

Can you see why? Even you would choose the second one wouldn't you?

If you can honestly look at your cover letter and know that it wouldn't appeal to you then you need to makes some changes. If you can objectively look at your cover letter, pretending that it was an application for Martha Jones or John Citizen and it jumped out to you wanting you to read more, than you've got something good there.

Always run it by friends and family, don't be so attached to your cover letter that you won't budge and makes some alterations along the way. The whole purpose of this exercise is to get you to craft the best cover letter possible and for it to get read. Put ego and emotions aside because you need to be flexible if you want to apply for an array of jobs.

Here are some power openers to use, mix and match them when creating your own cover letter. Having a good mix of these will get you noticed fast. They give your employer a reason to keep reading because you're bringing something of interest to the table.

Getting this practice is essential for crafting cover letters on the fly. Loosening up your brain allows you to write quickly and effectively which also comes in handy when hitting the interview, those skills will serve you well when quizzed by your employer.

7 POWER OPENERS TO COME OUT SWINGING WITH

Power Opener One:

"I was pleased when a position from your company became available. Looking at the criteria outlined in your job advertisement I have all of the expertise and skills you're looking for which is why I would like to get in touch with you so I can convince you in person."

Power Opener Two:

"I have saved my present company_____in potential lost revenue by improving system processes and time management issues increasing productivity by more than_____%.

I know I can do the same for your company."

Power Opener Three:

"I increased revenue for the company I formerly worked for and through my efforts was able add an extra $ _____in unexpected income."

Power Opener Four:

Although I have been out of the job market for a while raising my child, I have kept my finger on the pulse within the advertizing industry to include shifting market trends and extensive market research.

I have a portfolio of cutting edge ideas and techniques I would like to share with you in person to illustrate my findings. I believe it would be of great value to your company and to your bottom line.

Power Opener Five:

Being a homemaker for the past 3 years makes me more than qualified for the position of 2nd grade teacher. In addition to my full teaching certification I have acquired real world practical experience both within the home and within the classroom, which more than prepares me for the role.

Power Opener Six

By working for your direct competitor for the past 4 years I bring with me vast knowledge and experience that has enabled me to increase company sales by _____%, something I'm confident I can do for you.

I would like to meet with you face to face to discuss what I have in mind to boost your company growth and profits.

Power Opener Seven:

As media technology continues to change, you need someone who can learn rapidly and adapt at the same pace.
With extensive experience in the film and television industry and a degree in media studies, I have a lot to offer your company.

Special Note:

For the love of you and everything on this earth, don't put yourself down. It's difficult to take anyone seriously when you don't take yourself seriously. You have to project the kind of candidate they want and need while being honest and true to yourself at the same time.

When writing your cover letter stick to the usual fonts because they are the most common, recognizable and easiest to read.

WORDS TO AVOID

Knowing what to say is just important as knowing what to leave out. This is because certain words have the opposite effect of building you up such as the previous power phrases. They can actually leave hanging doubt in the back of your employers mind and hinder your chances. Words such as "hope", although a great word in its own right but included in the following phrase "I hope you will get back to me", or "I hope to meet with you". This leaves too much room for the unknown to occur. The word hope leaves the ball completely in the court of the employer, its gives them all the leverage and the power and doesn't earn you any respect.

You have to be proactive from your opening paragraph all the way to your conclusion expecting nothing less than a meeting with the employer. You can also show how serious you are by taking the initiative to call them. That way you're making something happen of your own accord and taking matters and your fate into your hands rather than to leave it in the laps of the employer gods.

So what are some of the words you should avoid? Stuffy, unnecessarily long words including words that cast any doubt over your abilities and suitability for the position.

Here are just a few words to avoid putting in your cover letter.

- I hope
- If I
- I think
- I believe
- I feel
- Perhaps
- Possibly
- Maybe
- Probably
- Might
- Could
- Should
- Concerned

- Liable
- Most likely
- Unlikely
- Doubt
- Hesitate
- Desperate
- Incapable
- Unsure
- Flaws
- Uncertain
- Unable
- Can't
- Fear

- Sorry
- Unhappy
- But
- However
- Disappointed
- Fired
- Hate
- Dislike
- Idle
- Weaknesses
- Shortcomings
- Lacking
- Deficient

- Really
- Chance
- Try
- Salary

These words are like Kryptonite to your cover letter they make you appear self doubting and unsure. Getting rid of these words will automatically make you sound more confident and self assured.

Here are a few examples of words that will help your cover letter pack a punch:

- Created
- Improved
- Refined
- Organized
- Orchestrated
- Planned
- Performed
- Exercised
- Encouraged
- Enabled
- Structured
- Streamlined
- Communicated
- Guided
- Led
- Managed
- Resolved
- Motivated
- Uplifted
- Eliminated
- Oversaw
- Executed
- Processed
- Improved
- Built
- Promoted
- Intuitively
- Debuted
- Introduced
- Publicized
- Governed
- Managed
- Handled

- Flourished
- Growth
- Delegated
- Allocated
- Facilitated
- Trained

- Coached
- Merged
- Incited
- Driven
- Prompted
- Generated

- Instructed
- Monitored
- Spearheaded
- Assembled
- Obtained

A WORD ABOUT FONTS

Try to avoid using freaky fonts or serif fonts, comic sans, mistral and anything that tries to mimic natural handwriting. It's ok to experiment but keep within the required font types because if employers have any difficulty in reading your cover letter it won't get the chance it deserves. So don't let a bad font type cost you the job.

Try going for the most common fonts like:

- Times new Roman
- Courier
- Arial
- Verdana

Font size 12 is the usual standard.

THE LETTER TYPES

There are 4 basic letter types which are designed to suit the part of application process you're at.

Here are the 4 main cover letter types along with some real world examples to give you an idea of how it works.

Cover Letter Types

You will discover different sets of cover letter types depending upon which part of the job application process you find yourself at.

These main cover letters are:

- **Snail Mail Letter And Email Response For Employment Vacancy**
- **Take The Bull By The Horns Cover Letter**
- **Thank You Letter**
- **Follow Up Letter**

1. Snail Mail Letter And Email Response For Advertized Vacancy

Is the template of choice when applying for a job position, naturally you include the details of the vacancy you are applying for and when you saw the job advertised.

It works equally well as a physical snail mail cover letter or as an email, however in email version, don't try to hype up your subject line for the purpose of getting noticed. If there's anything to by don't use the words in your subject line such as "Read this!" "Must Open". Use these blacklisted words and no doubt your e-cover letter will never see the light of day once it's immediately filtered into the spam folder.

Place the name of the person it's addressed to along with it's purpose, i.e. "Job

Application", that way it won't get filtered into the junk folder abyss never to be seen again.

Feel free to send both email and snail mail versions, that way should one get lost you at least have a back up.

Don't be afraid to get a little creative here, and winners get full points for doing so. Avoid the stagnant beaten path when it comes to the usual token default response that comes with most cover letter templates. That's why these cover letters have all been written specifically to grab instant attention, because you're going to need it.

Use these templates, modify them, and make them your own. It should after all reflect you. Make them want to know more about you within the first few seconds and to do that, be creative, think outside the square. Don't do what everyone else does and that's to plug their contact details into the same old drab cover letters everyone and their dog else has. Paint a picture of yourself with your words and hook them straight out of the gate.

Not sure how to? refer back to the "You're Hired!" manual, practice writing killer openings and the rest will come.

Refer to these cover letters to get a feel for the openers, you'll notice none of them rest on their laurels and hope that the resume gets read. You can't rely on that. You always have to believe that your cover letter is it, it fails to get read and you won't even get the job, let alone the interview.

2. Take The Bull By The Horns Cover Letter

The Take The Bull By The Horns cover letter implies just that. This is the type of cover letter that doesn't require waiting for the perfect job position to appear. You would use this type of cover letter you would use to break the ice and to let the employer know who you are. It also shows that you're confident and have taken the initiative to get the job you want. Your resume may only end up on file but on the flipside you also have the chance of getting the job you really want.

You're putting your job feelers out there to see what's happening in the job market and to try your luck.

All is fair in love, war and job hunting. Just because a job vacancy you're particularly eyeballing hasn't presented itself doesn't mean that vacancies for it aren't available. The majority of jobs aren't advertised so your persistence and diligence will pay off.

3. The Thank You Letter

Everything these days is about making an impression and we've become so engrossed in ourselves that we often forget to say thank you. A thank you letter is imperative after sending in your cover letter or for following up after an interview. Even when you receive a rejection letter it's all about being thankful for the opportunity and making a lasting impression long after the interview. Research shows that the more contact you have after just the initial cover letter will lock you into their memory banks. A cover letter followed by a thank you letter for the interview and for the rejection speaks volumes about your character and your attitude.

As they say, your aptitude plus your attitude equals your altitude. In other words, how you handle rejection will ultimately determine how far you go whether it be job wise or in life, this principle still applies. That's another point that sets the winners apart from the losers, something as simple as their attitude, which is something we all have control over no matter what our circumstances are financial or otherwise. So don't be afraid to give out a thank you letter even when they reject you. Trust me, hardly anyone is doing this after taking it personally and feeling jilted and like you've just had another pin added in your balloon.

Don't take rejection personally, it takes a certain amount of rejection to hit the successes and only those who know this enjoy the spoils of victory while everyone else falls by the way side long before they ever get to taste its sweetness.

4. The Follow Up Letter

Just as the name implies, the Follow Up letter is to keep in contact with your employer. It also kick-starts any cold leads or contacts, activity that has hit a dead end.

This helps to job their memory of you and to revive the contact. Although they may have closed the vacancy which may have been why contact went dead, it's still a good idea to show you're keen should the next job position become available Envelopes send messages too

Email vs. Snail Mail Cover Letter

How to Create Attention Grabbing Subject Lines

If in doubt, send both. That way you doubly ensure they receive it, they see that you're keen and you've cornered both mediums.

There are a couple of differences between paper cover letters and electronic ones, for instance the subject line is extremely important when it comes to grabbing attention.

Some don'ts – just like with spam, you don't want your subject line to appear hyped up or deceptive for the purpose of getting read. This will annoy and infuriate, the beauty of the delete button is it simplicity to delete junk with a single click. That means avoiding words like **"Read This!", "Open Now!"** Especially with exclamation marks will only get your cover letter filtered into the spam folder before your employer ever gets the chance to see it. You don't need to use gimmicks or trickery to get attention, if anything resorting to those types of tactics will only work against you.

To ensure your e-cover letter doesn't end up as e-waste write something like **"Attention Brent Spiner – Job Application For Media Position",** the most important thing to remember with subject lines is that you have such limited space. It's important to put the most relevant information upfront, not only will get attention from the appropriate person but the purpose is clearly stated separating it from the rest of the spam and junk mail.

DON'T CAPITALIZE to get attention as it's the written equivalent of shouting.

Make sure it goes to the correct person, if you're unsure, contact the company personally and get the necessary information.

YOUR PLAN OF ATTACK – PUTTING IT ALL INTO ACTION

Napoleon Bonaparte had his and now so will you.

Every success has had behind it a plan, a blueprint that was acted upon.

You need the same, this is where it all comes together for you, and most people won't even have a plan of attack. They'll just mail out to whatever job takes their fancy and this may be few and far between and they wonder why they don't get any results. This is because they don't have a strategy. If you fail to plan you plan to fail.

Treat this as a direct mail campaign. Direct mailers believe in the numbers game. The more baited fishhooks sitting in the water, the more fish they'll catch, the trick is to keep the unique personal touch suited to each particular job position.

You need a plan to succeed and it's this strategy that will ultimately get you noticed over all others.

I know this may seem like a lot but if you can go the extra mile and show your dedication, you are revealing a lot about your character and the kind of person that you are and whether you realize now or not, this will help you to stand out and will be remembered.

If you're prepared to do what 99% of others aren't, you'll be scooping up the lion share of the jobs. So persevere, it will pay off.

Cover Letter Checklist and Little Extras To Remember

Does your cover letter state the purpose of writing?

Have you included how you found the company's advertized job position? If you're cold calling state why you're choosing that particular company to apply to.

Have you listed your most pertinent skills, experience and qualifications at the beginning of your application to strengthen your application?

Do your qualifications and skills match the job you're applying for?

✔ Have you included all relevant skills and jobs for the position you'reapplying for?

✔ Did you remember to include all relevant achievements?

✔ Does your first paragraph come out swinging? Does it grab the attention of the reader to want to read more?

✔ Does what follows in the remaining paragraphs support your first paragraph?

✔ Keep in line with the same theme by using the same paper for your coverletter, resume and your envelope.

✔ Have you included your contact details?

✔ Are you sending your cover letter to the correct person, department and company? If in doubt, research the necessary details online or call the company for verification.

✔ Have you checked for spelling and grammar errors?

✔ Have you typed everything? the only thing that should be handwritten is your signature only.

✓ Does your cover letter make an impression? does it jump off the page? Does it achieve what it sets out to do? Ask your family and friends for their feedback.

✓ Is the tone, wording in your cover letter simple and to the point? not stilted or flowery? Did you use any technical language or jargon that would confuse those not familiar with it such as recruiters?

✓ Have you included your strengths and how those can benefit the company you're applying to?

✓ Does your cover letter end with a proactive conclusion? a pledge to follow up with the employer or to arrange a meeting in person?

So there you have it, all the tips and tricks to start getting those jobs.

Follow this, always improving and refining your cover letters and you'll turn your luck around in your favor and start getting those jobs you've been missing out on.

Now go out there and get them!
OK, so now you're ready to write your cover letter.
Here are some killer templates, written expressly for you.
You're closer to getting those jobs now.

COVER LETTER TEMPLATES

A Quick Note:

Remember to personalize these cover letter templates and to make them your own, each application should reflect your personality.

Remember, these are just guidelines designed to give you an outline to work to. Let your cover letter represent you and your personality always bearing in mind that the first paragraph is the most important and crucial one to make an impression.

Like writing a classified ad, you only have a small amount of space to make a memorable impression in, so make the most of it. It certainly doesn't hurt to put your best out there straight off the bat and that includes your greatest achievements, not only is it bold but it says a lot about the person saying it. You're different, don't mind using your initiative and aren't afraid to take risks. Hard „em hard and hit „em fast.

When you read these cover letter templates you won't find the usual stale ones you see sitting on the library shelves or floating endlessly in cyberspace. These cover letters are unique, punchy and attention getting and were designed to grab your employers eyes within the first 8 seconds, better than any other cover letter course can boast. Your employer will be glued before they even get a chance to move onto the next cover letter on the pile. Not only will it demand attention but it will have them reaching for the phone to call you.

While other cover letters are dispensing with the niceties and the formal introduction that will frankly put an insomniac to sleep, yours will grab them by the eyes where they'll want to find out more about you. Don't worry, if they're interested, they want to know, just make sure you have your contact details ready so that phone will ring.

It makes sense, I mean think about it, they read the first and only paragraph, you might as well sock it to them there and then, that way you greatly increase your odds of them reading the rest and calling you for the interview. You've got nothing to lose.

If they don't call, they don't call. The more failures the closer you get to the successes.

So just like a sales letter, experiment with what works until you finally achieve your personal best in terms of your pick of the bunch of the best jobs. Get to the point - you've got to hook them and fast, always think 8 seconds and you'll never waste another second again.

With cover letters like these, your employer won't be able to resist and you will be giving your competition a run for their money. Now get that job!

TEMPLATE ONE:

Snail Mail Letter And Email Response For Advertized Vacancy

(Position of Sales Representative) Dear Mr. Neville,

Being personally responsible for increasing revenue from $50,000 per month to

$100,000 per month within an 18-month timeframe for the last firm I worked for, I find myself ready for a new challenge and would like the opportunity to bring my skills and expertise to your company to produce similar, if not better results.

What drew me to apply for the position advertised in the on

_____ was that your company's values and core beliefs tie in with my own and I believe I would be a good fit to both your business and a valuable member of the team.

On my attached resume you will find:

Strong background in Sales and Marketing with an MBA from _

_____ 3 years of practical experience within the sales realm

Managed a sales team of 5 resulting in increased company revenue Spearheaded several projects resulting in increased company profits

I know I have more to learn and gain from you and your company and welcome the challenge. I also know that the knowledge and experience I have already gained will be a valuable asset to your company.

I would like to meet with you in person to discuss matters further and look forward to an interview at your earliest convenience.

Yours sincerely,

Albert Brooks (555)-xxx-xxx
youremail@youremailhere.com

TEMPLATE TWO:

Snail Mail Letter And Email Response For Advertized Vacancy (Position of Teaching Staff)

Dear Mrs. Miller,

If you're looking for a hard working, trustworthy and self-reliant employee who is a fully certified Grade 3 teacher then I believe I am the person for the job.

I am applying for the position found in the_____ dated

_____.

My qualifications, experience, work ethic and personality make me a natural fit for the position.

Being a teacher for the past 5 years I have gained an extensive working knowledge of the education system, creating and structuring lesson plans, orchestrating meetings where the needs of the children are concerned, formed rapport with family members and are aware of cultural sensitivities and protocol for each individual situation.

I would like the opportunity to bring my skills, knowledge and experience where I feel they would be of benefit to your

100

students. I am also keen to continually upgrade my skills when the need arises so that I will always be able to offer my best.

Enclosed in my application you will find a copy of my resume. I would like to meet in person with you to discuss this matter in further detail.

Look forward to meeting with you. Sincere regards,

Sally Michaels (555)-xxx-xxx

youremail@youremailhere.com

TEMPLATE THREE:

Snail Mail Letter And Email Response For Advertized Vacancy (Position of Legal Administrator)

Dear Ms. Roberts,

Hard working, dedicated, loyal and trustworthy are just some of the qualities that I possess that I feel will be of value to your company. I am applying for the position of Legal Administrator, found in_____ on the _____.

For the past 2 years I have worked as a legal administrator for one very high profile, respected firm.

During that time I gained relevant experience within the industry and quickly built up a rapport amongst my peers. I was in a position to hone my people skills enabling me to juggle a variety of situations which only served to make me a better listener and organizer, skills which I believe will be an investment to your company.

I have experience in time management, am efficient in the followingcomputer packages___, _____and _____and knowledge of accounting packages that has saved thousands of dollars by keeping this task in house.

I would like to meet with you at your earliest convenience and am requesting an interview with you.

Enclosed you will contact details and my attached resume for your perusal. With kind regards,

Michael Green (555)-xxx-xxx

youremail@youremailhere.com

TEMPLATE FOUR:

Snail Mail Letter And Email Response For Advertized Vacancy (Position of Investment Banker)

Dear Mr. Kennelly,

I was keen to learn that recently a position had opened within your firm for Investment Banker and would like to apply for the position advertized on the_____.

Reading the requirements I feel I'm the ideal candidate for the job. I am computer literate and have extensive knowledge in relevant software applications. Through company training, all of the usual outsourced tasks are now managed in house, adding thousands of dollars in revenue through savings. I alone saved the company an extra $20,000 per year.

I am trustworthy, sensitive and conduct myself in a professional manner at all times. I'm a people person and have a keen sense of humor allowing me to connect with people and make them feel at ease, I believe this is an integral part of what has made me such a successful team player. I also have a passion and a genuine interest for the job and welcome a new challenge, I feel of which I will get with your firm.

I am writing to arrange a meeting with you in person so that we can discuss matters in further detail.

Appreciate your time. Sincerely,

James Mason (555)-123-4567

youremail@youremailhere.com

TEMPLATE FIVE:

Snail Mail Letter And Email Response For Advertized Vacancy (Position of Human Resources Officer)

Dear Mr. Williams,

Currently employed as a Human Resources manager I already have the pertinent qualifications required for the position advertised_____ and would be a perfect fit for your company.

Looking at your company's core beliefs which I share myself and upon speaking with your recruiter _____on the_____he/she encouraged me to put in my resume feeling that my skills and credentials tie in well with your companies core beliefs and values.

Enclosed is my application, you will also find my resume with my most relevant education, experience and employment history disclosed.

Here are just a few of my skills and attributes to consider for the position.

• Highly focused and goal orientated team leader who always reaches and excels performance targets.

- Ability to mobilize team with my people skills motivating them to achievetarget goals.
- Able to time manage with efficiency and execute and accomplish any project within the set deadline especially with regards to time critical projects.
- Successfully identified and solved problems during the project development phase before they became major setbacks, saving thousands of dollars in potential losses.
- Experience in Human Resources administration and support services.
- Sound knowledge and competence in the relevant administrative tools and applications

Possess team leadership qualities and experience but also do well as part of a team. I would like to further discuss this with you in detail and would like to request an interview.

TEMPLATE SIX:

Snail Mail Letter And Email Response For Advertized Vacancy (Position of Office Administrator)

Dear Ms Blakely,

Your position for Office Administrator stood out to me in particular because my skills and experience tie in perfectly with what your company is looking for. I'm so confident that my experience is closely aligned with your company's requirements that you need to get in touch with me so that I can explain in greater detail why I'm the only person for the job.

I am responsible for improving office processes and productivity in particular where time management is critical, reducing the amount of wasted downtime and inefficient practices overall has saved money.

I am a good communicator and ensure that information is forwarded and received safely by the appropriate channels.

I am trustworthy and handle client details and file information with the utmost respect and confidentiality.

Through my passion for the job and for people has given me excellent communication and people skills where I enjoy interacting with staff and clientele.

TEMPLATE SEVEN:

Take The Bull By The Horns Cover Letter (Position of Sales Manager)

Dear Mr. Smith,

After generating sales in excess of 3 million dollars for the company I am currently employed with I feel that after 7 years I am ready for the next challenge and have got my sights set on your company, particularly because I my current skill set is a good fit for your organization and I have much to offer.

I would like to take the opportunity to explain exactly why I would make the perfect candidate for your company.

Upon _____ recommendation over the phone I was encouraged to send in my resume as he/she deemed me to be a good fit for the organization and in line with what your company is currently looking for.

My credentials for the position include:

• Established and handpicked a sales team responsible for a 22% sales increase, additional revenue that was generated as a direct result of my actions

- Implemented full staff training to get them up to speed with company product knowledge.
- Increased brand recognition and global market penetration that saw an overall 12% increase in global market share.

I would like to arrange a meeting with you in person so that I discuss matters with you in more detail and appreciate your consideration.

Look forward to your reply. Sincerely,

Owen Jacobs (555)-xxx-xxx

TEMPLATE EIGHT:

Take The Bull By The Horns Cover Letter (Position of Media Specialist)

Dear Mr. Jones

I realize that currently there are no openings within your organization for a media specialist however there are a few things about me I would like to bring to your attention.

- I was personally responsible for overhauling our entire cataloguing system making it more efficient, saving in hundreds of wasted man-hours.

- I saved over 11% in extra funds that would have been spent as a result of unnecessary over time as was required with the old system.

- I was responsible for the selection and purchasing of 2 million dollars worth of new books for the library I currently work for.

- I am an experienced librarian and currently hold a bachelors degree in library media education from the University of Chicago.

Although I am still currently employed at my current job I would like the chance to work for your organization because it has always been a dream of mine.

I have increased my current employers efficiency and created extra funds from by implementing more efficient systems and feel that I can do the same for you.

I would like to discuss matters with you in more detail and appreciate being considered for a future role of media specialist within your company.

Yours sincerely,

Angela Brown. (555)-xxx-xxx
youremail@youremailhere.com

TEMPLATE NINE:

Thank You Letter

Dear Mr. Jenkins,

I am grateful for the time you took out of your busy schedule to meet with me on_____and appreciate the opportunity to discuss the job role in further detail.

I thank you for the suggestions you put forth during our meeting and am informing you that I have taken your advice and implemented it.

I have updated my resume accordingly in line with your suggestions and have enclosed the updated version with this letter.

You will notice that I have updated my job performance to better reflect the position applied for to include:

- _____
- _____
- _____

I look forward to hearing from you at your earliest convenience.

With kind regards.

Alan Simpson (555)-xxx-xxx

youremail@youremailhere.com

TEMPLATE TEN:

Follow Up Letter

Dear Mr. Robinson,

I enjoyed our meeting today and appreciate the time you took to interview me.

As we discussed in the interview I know that my experience, skills and qualifications make me the ideal person for the position and after talking over matters in further detail realize even more that I can have a lot to offer and bring to the job.

I will follow up with you on __

Sincerely,

Sara Mitchell (555)-xxx-xxx

youremail@youremailhere.com

9 786069 836408

Printed by Libri Plureos GmbH in Hamburg, Germany